How Kittens Grow

by MILLICENT E. SELSAM

Photographs by ESTHER BUBLEY

SCHOLASTIC BOOK SERVICES
NEW YORK · TORONTO · LONDON · AUCKLAND · SYDNEY · TOKYO

ISBN: 0-590-04794-9

22 21 20 19 18 17 16 15 14 13   1 2 3 4 5 6/8
Printed in the U.S.A.   07

The author wishes to thank Dr. Jay S. Rosenblatt, Professor of Psychology, Institute of Animal Behavior, Rutgers State University, for reading the manuscript of this book.

Mother cat has just given birth to these four kittens.
She lies on her side and licks them off.

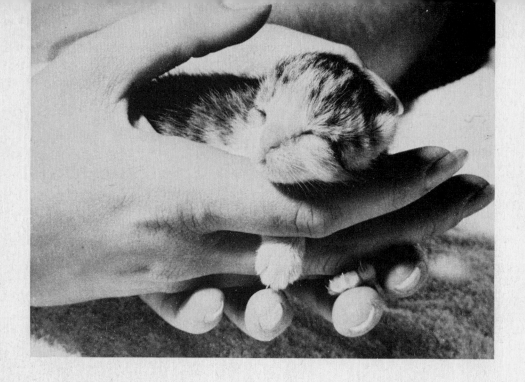

Each kitten is tiny.

It cannot see because its eyes are closed.

It cannot hear because its ears are still closed.

But the kitten can smell, and touch, and feel warmth.

Each kitten crawls towards
its mother's warm body.
Its front legs move forward slowly.
It drags its hind legs along.
Its head moves from side to side.
At last it reaches mother cat.

Now the kitten nuzzles in mother cat's fur
with its nose and mouth.
It keeps nuzzling until it touches a nipple.
Then it grabs the nipple with its mouth
and begins to suck milk.
Each kitten sucks milk within an hour after it is born.

These tiny kittens need their mother.

She nurses them.

She keeps them warm.

She keeps them safe.

For two days mother cat stays with the kittens
almost all the time.
About every two hours she gets up.
She stretches.
Then she goes off to eat something.

After the second day, she gets up more often.
The kittens sleep while she is away.
They usually sleep on top of one another.
They keep warm that way.

When mother cat comes back, she licks the kittens.
This wakes them up.
Then mother cat lies down
and the kittens suck milk again.

By this time each kitten has learned to nurse
at its own special nipple.
If another kitten tries to take its place,
it holds on tight and will not let go.

When the kittens are about a week old,
their eyes begin to open.
But they cannot see much.
Their ears are open now too.
But they cannot hear very much.

The kittens are growing.
They weigh twice as much now
as they weighed when they were born.

At two weeks, the kittens still crawl.

They cannot walk yet.

But they are beginning to see more and hear more.

Sometimes a kitten crawls
away from its mother.
But then the floor feels cold.
And the floor smells different.
The kitten cries.
Mother cat hears it.
She goes to it and carries it home by the neck.

Now the kittens are three weeks old.

They can go over to the mother cat to nurse
when she does not come to them.

They try to stand on their feet and walk a little.

Each week they gain about six ounces.

At four weeks the kittens are walking slowly.

They are still wobbly on their feet.

But they see pretty well.

And they hear very well.

Mother cat goes to the kittens less and less.
But the kittens can follow her around now,
and make her lie down and let them nurse.
They still nurse at their own special nipples.

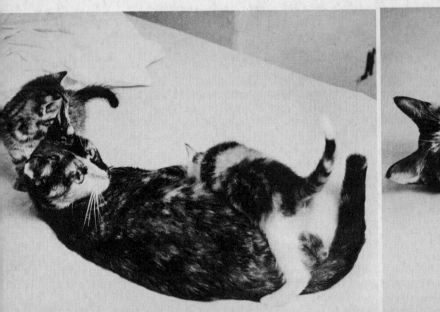

Now the kittens can play with each other.

They lick each other.

They chase each other.

They roll over each other.

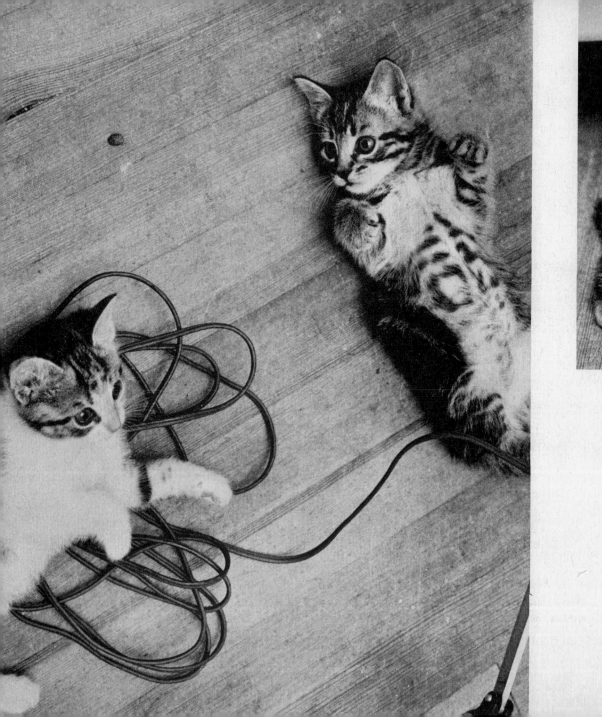

They play with
everything they can find.

They run after mother cat.

They jump on her.

They lick her face.

They bite her tail.

Sometimes the playing
gets too rough.
Then mother cat jumps
away from the kittens.
She jumps on a high stool,
or up to a shelf.
Sometimes she swats the kittens.

When the kittens are five weeks old,
they are getting less milk from their mother.
But they can drink milk from a saucer.

They follow mother cat when she goes to feed.

Sometimes they step in the food dish.

Sometimes they step on some food on the floor.

Then they lick their paws.

The food tastes good!

Sometimes they lick the mother's mouth

and taste the food that way.

That is how they learn to eat solid food.

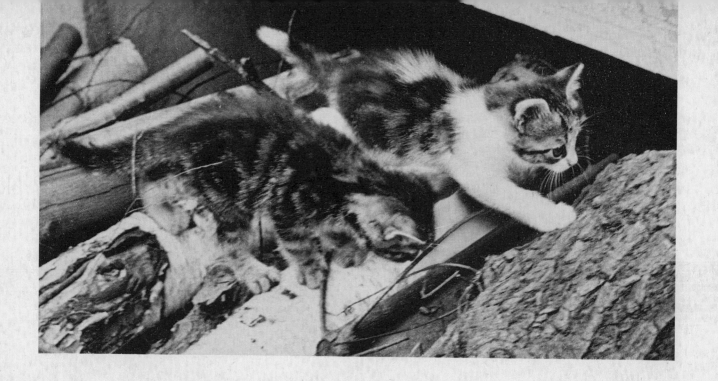

On farms, cats hunt their own food.
At first, mother cat brings live animals
back to the kittens.
They learn to know the food they will later
hunt themselves.
Then the kittens begin to follow the mother when
she goes to find food.

That is how they learn to hunt
and kill small animals, especially mice.
The kittens have teeth now and can chew.
These are baby teeth at first, just as yours are.
When a cat is about six months old, the baby
teeth fall out and the adult teeth
take their place.

When the kittens are about eight weeks old,
they have stopped getting milk from their mother.
They have learned to eat solid food.
They can chase, climb, leap, run, move quietly
through the grass, and pounce on a mouse.

They can do everything a grown-up cat can do.
This is the best time to get a kitten.